SexTherapy 101

By Dr. Debra Laino

SexTherapy 101

Dr. Debra Laino

© 2013, Dr. Debra Laino

No part of this publication may be reproduced or transmitted in any form or by any means, mechanical or electronic, including photocopying and recording, or by any information storage and retrieval system, without permission in writing from the publisher. Requests for permission or further information should be addressed to the publishers.

ISBN-13: 978-1494750565
ISBN-10: 1494750562

This book is dedicated to all the individuals and couples who need help in the area of sexuality and relationships.

I also want to graciously thank my partner and best friend Robert for his continued support throughout my chaotic schedule, random ideas, and stubbornness.

CONTENTS

Foreword	xi
Introduction	1
Improving Your Relationship One Step at a Time	5
Are You Lacking Desire? (Female Edition)	33
Are You Lacking Desire? (Male Edition)	47
Erectile "Dys"function Quick Tips	55
Getting Control Over Premature Ejaculation	65
How to Talk to Your Young Children About Sexuality	83
Summary	97

Foreword

When you Google "Sex Therapy," there are 86,200,200 page links returned in 0.34 seconds. It is simply mind boggling that so much material is already available on this subject. Even with everything that has been written about sex and sex therapy, there is still room for one more book on this subject. In my opinion, *Sex Therapy 101* fits this bill well.

I am writing this Foreword because Dr. Debra Laino is the real deal and this book is a truly legitimate guide to finally help you understand the difference between "intimacy" and "sexual intimacy." For those who are reluctant to even say the word "sex therapy," or even consider going to a sex therapist like Dr. Laino, this is a great guidebook.

As the organizer of TEDxWilmington, I invited Dr. Laino to speak at the 2013 TEDxWilmington. I found her to be a powerful speaker who could tackle a challenging subject and make it fun and accessible to the audience. I invite you to watch her TEDx talk which was entitled "Low libido. Prime Your Pump Ladies" on:

http://youtube/PRfONo0O6Po.

It is a great idea to learn what works and what doesn't work from an expert. This book is written by a board certified clinical sexologist and sex therapist in layman's language. Invest the time to read it carefully so that you can reap the benefits from all this expert guidance. Enjoy this journey and remove the obstacles to intimacy.

Ajit Mathew George
Organizer, TEDxWilmington

Introduction

Welcome to my book. Chances are, if you purchased this book, you are seeking some guidance in your relationship. Well, you've come to the right place. I work with many couples on a daily basis, helping them improve their relationships. I created this book to help couples get back on track—and specifically for those individuals who are apprehensive about coming into a doctor's office for therapy, either because of financial reasons, or due to embarrassment, and/or any of the other reasons couples may decide not to make an appointment with a therapist.

While it may be true that some relationships include individuals who are incompatible, other couples just need a little assistance, and I have found this assistance usually comes in three forms:

1) Better Communication

2) Increased Intimacy
3) Better Sex

Yes, getting better at these three simple things can positively affect your relationship. My goal is to help you increase your understanding, and in turn your skill levels, in these areas. Since the changes we are talking about here usually involve many *small steps* rather than a few *huge leaps*, I have included a section on "Improving Your Relationship One Step at a Time." The remaining sections of this book address desire—or, more specifically, the *lack* of desire—for both male and female, and finally I address erectile dysfunction. In chapter 6, I've included a section that gives guidance on talking to your young children about sexuality, a topic most readers will find valuable.

The Exercises

For many readers, a bit more interaction with the material may be required to get the full value from this content; simply reading the sections of this book isn't enough. I hope you will do the work to complete the basic exercises found throughout this manual, and that you will gain the skills needed for a healthy, satisfying relationship.

I've found that some people never take action because they are uncomfortable with such topics, or they feel awkward with the idea of seeing a therapist. That doesn't have to be the end. For example, if visiting a therapist's office is a concern for you or your mate, one thing you can do—and it's the same thing I'd have you do if you came into my office—is work on the exercises. Then reflect on your thoughts, feelings, and reactions to the exercises. You can do this in the privacy of your own home by way of writing (i.e. in a journal), or you can work on these exercises together out loud in a comfortable setting. And remember: I'm here if you need me!

Dr. Debra Laino

1
Improving Your Relationship One Step at a Time

What Is A Relationship?

Though you may think you already know the answer to this question, it may not be defined as you have been taught.

A relationship is generally defined as a *close interpersonal relationship*. This leads to the question of what an interpersonal relationship is and is it the same as an *intra*-personal relationship? Having an intimate relationship plays a central role in being human. There is solid research on this, supporting the idea that "isolation" is detrimental; having a life devoid of relationships (any kind, really) has a negative effect on humans. Furthermore, it is reinforced again in everyday life that humans have a need to *belong*, a need to love and to be loved. We originally get into relationships with people we like and with whom we are attracted to in some way.

> **Definition**
>
> **"Intra"** – a prefix meaning "within" and used in compound words such as intrastate (which means "within a state" and may refer to travel that does not cross the border).

I want to break this down for you in a little more detail.

Let's focus on three types of relationships: Interpersonal, Intra-personal, and Intimate relationships.

1) *Interpersonal Relationships* are relationships with other people or another person with whom we are attracted to in some way, or in multiple ways.

2) An *Intra-Personal Relationship* is the relationship we have with ourselves.

3) The term *Intimate Relationship* is often used euphemistically to describe a sexual relationship. But there is so much more; these are interpersonal relationships with a high level of intimacy, both sexual and non-sexual intimacy. These types of relationships also involve intrapersonal relationships; the healthiest relationships are made up of people who have a good amount of self-awareness of the fact that they like themselves.

> **Definition**
>
> **"Inter"** – a prefix meaning "between" and used in compound words such as interstate (which mean "between states" and may refer to travel that crosses the border).

Intimacy and Sexual Intimacy

If you are anything like me, you may wonder what the difference is between *intimacy* and *sexual intimacy*. Please know there is a difference, and I will help you to understand that difference. I often see people misconstrue these meanings. To be quite honest, in my practice and experience, I see more men that have a difficult time with the meaning of intimacy than women, but this misconception is not necessary for any of us. Let's clear that up before we go any further.

Intimacy (often referred to as emotional intimacy) is simply defined as:

The sharing of thoughts and feelings

Intimacy differs from sexual intimacy. Sexual intimacy not only consists of the sharing of thoughts and feelings (goals, hopes, etc. for the future), but it goes beyond that and moves into the physical realm. It includes the sexual body, mind, and spirit connection. This extra step is, for obvious reasons, key to sexual intimacy.

A difference between men and women, with regard to these two concepts, exists and is illustrated in the way that males and females use the terms differently. Men learn that to be "intimate" is to have sex. This is often how men feel loved and how they relate to being important to their partner. In contrast, women learn that to be "intimate" means to be listened to, acknowledged, and to be "number one" in her partner's life. The divide here is that females often do not relate the two types of intimacy but rather separate the two dichotomies.

That being said, there is a tremendous need for couples to be educated about this subtle (but often profound) difference so that each person can understand the individuality of their partner and in turn grow their definitions both individually and together. This can be done by making the effort to understand where your partner is coming from and by identifying the differences between the ways you and your partner think. I help couples expand and merge their definitions. It is this merging that helps couples bridge their differences in thinking. I always tell my clients that you are *both* right and you are *both* wrong in this realm. You are right for yourself and the process is learning to become right for your partner, too. Understanding and then applying that understanding to your own behavior is the key.

Why People Get Into Relationships

As stated above, people get into relationships because of a human need to "connect." We generally like the person and are attracted to them; and we often move forward into a sexual realm. However, this isn't always the case. Take for example Bill:

Bill, a 35-year-old male, was divorced and emotionally wounded from his failed marriage. Because of the path his marriage had taken, and the anger he felt, he was not going to enter into another relationship in the same way.

Smart move, right?

Well, not so much. Bill decided that he did not want to be attracted to the next person to the extent he had been attracted to his first wife. This was the source of his pain after all. His first wife had engaged in numerous affairs and was emotionally disconnected from him, yet Bill still tried in the marriage. There were dependency, codependency, self-esteem, and self-worth issues that Bill needed to work on. After the divorce, Bill met a woman who he became very good friends with—he noted that he was not attracted to her physically at all; rather, he fell in love with the *companionship* and the *friendship*, which he did not have in his first marriage. They got married, and ten years into the marriage they reported having had sex 10 times throughout their marriage. Bill realized he got married the second time for the wrong reasons—basically because he was hurt during his first marriage.

What happened to Bill, and his second wife, is irrelevant at this point. The story of Bill highlights one of the many different reasons people get into relationships. Focus for a moment on the following question:

What are the reasons you got into your current relationship?

For many people, the answer(s) to this question might lead to many other questions—and many insights also.

 Exercise: *"Reflection"*

Reflection Exercise: Take a moment and think about

the reasons you decided to get into your relationship. Why were you attracted to your partner? You will most likely find that you were attracted on several levels. Were you lonely? Were you good friends?

For now, don't worry about the meaning behind these questions. I just want you to identify the answer(s).

Even if you got into your relationship lacking entirely rational reasons, that's OK. You can still have a solid relationship built on trust, understanding, and an emotional/physical connection. This reflection exercise is just to bring some awareness to you. I ask all of my clients how they met, what they liked about each other at the time, and what the feelings were like in the beginning. This is a good time to ask yourself these questions too. If you are using a journal... write these things down.

Is Your Relationship Struggling?

Chances are you purchased this book because your relationship is struggling, or at a minimum, you want to find some techniques to enhance the relationship. Most of us can identify at least one area of our intimate relationship that bothers us. Struggles in relationships aren't a bad thing; rather, the deciding factor of good versus bad is *how* the struggles are dealt with and resolved.

There are common signs a relationship is struggling. Those signs are generally as follows:

1. Distance (both emotional and physical)

Increased *emotional distance* creates an issue with *intimacy*. For some reason (every relationship is different) the talking and emotional sharing starts to diminish when a relationship is struggling. Communication falters, and the two of you are not discussing much on a personal level anymore.

In a similar fashion, increased *physical distance* creates an issue with sexual *intimacy*. Sexual intimacy is an important part of a relationship, and even though the sex drives of individuals vary, a lack of sexual intimacy is something that often needs to be worked through. Sex that used to be a once-a-week "enjoyment" has now turned to a once-every-three-months "occurrence." Most often, I hear couples speak of the amount of "effort" they have to put into having a sexual experience. This is a red flag in any relationship, a telltale sign that needs are not being met in the relationship…and happiness is waning.

2. Not enjoying each other's company

When the two of you got together you were probably all over one another with interest in everything the other one did. *What happened?* Oftentimes, when communication breaks down, resentment starts to build. Subsequently, when resentment builds, partners often lose enjoyment in being with one another.

3. Negative comments, said to each other

When negative comments override positive comments between two people, there is a big problem in the relationship. Negative comments signal distaste for one another. There are many research articles that discuss negative comments and their impact on relationships. As a matter of fact, one body of research states that there is a correlation between divorce and the ratio of negative to positive comments within a relationship. Common sense should dictate that the more loving the relationship, the more a couple makes loving comments to one another.

Let's not overlook sarcasm. Sarcasm is a dangerous playground for couples. Though it can be fun to "play" with one another, oftentimes sarcastic comments are taken to heart. Furthermore, they can become part of the communication style of the relationship. This has to stop. When I notice this with couples, I have them work hard on clearing up the communication with one another, because, as many of us know, there are usually bits of truth to sarcasms.

Definition
"Sarcasm" — a sharp, satirical expression, with sometimes opposite meaning, and often delivered using inflections in the voice.

4. Increased arguing with no resolve

Arguing is not necessarily a detriment to a relationship. You can be taught how to argue effectively and it can actually be healthy. All arguing indicates is that the two of you see things differently. This can be an area where couples can actually grow. There are general rules to arguing that I teach my clients:

    a) No name calling.
    b) Use "I" statements (to avoid blaming the other). Blame only puts people on the defensive, and an instant "battle of wills" ensues.
    c) Stay on the topic you have a disagreement about.

d) Don't "sandblast" (bringing up everything he or she ever did to you).

e) Listen to what your partner is saying (this involves the appropriate body language of facing your partner and looking at them). I often hear people say they are listening when, in fact, they are multitasking. Understand this: You are not giving your partner the undivided attention they deserve if you are doing something else or if you are thinking in your head about your response to what was said.

f) Acknowledge your partner's feelings. Right, wrong, or otherwise, your partner has feelings, and they need to be heard; whether you agree or not is not the issue. Your partner's feelings are valid and they have a right to feel that way.

Remember this: The one who wins the argument is irrelevant. If the argument damages your relationship—nothing is won.

Let's really get started...

Three Simple Ways to Improve Your Relationship
1) Communication

The first part of this book is about learning how to communicate effectively. Above are some points about arguing (a through f), which are also important functions of *communication*. This is because disagreements are inevitable. Contrary to popular belief, conflict is not a bad thing. Healthy conflict has to do with negotiation and collaboration, while unhealthy conflict has more to do with power and control. Conflict simply means we think differently on different things. Understanding and acknowledging those differences is key to learning how to deal with conflict. Oftentimes we get into *WILL battles* because we want our partner to think or feel the way we do on something. This activity needs to be let go of. People can be in loving, caring relationships even if they feel and think differently about things.

The platform for any healthy relationship—be it friend, sibling, parent, colleague, or romantic partner—is good communication. Funny thing is we communicate successfully every day with a multitude of people around us, but oftentimes we miss the mark when communicating effectively with our partner.

I once heard someone say, *"I do all the same things at work that I do in my (romantic) relationship and my colleagues like me a lot!"*

I had to chuckle at this, because it reflects a common misconception: "If I communicate well at work, I can communicate at home."

This couldn't be further from the truth. Work relationships and romantic-partner relationships are distinctly different relationships. Yes, even the media inspired, "work spouse," coined after someone realized how

Improving Your Relationship One Step at a Time

much time we actually spend at work.

Realize and accept that your intimate relationship is very different than all other relationships; the difference is marked. There is more emotional investment as well as sexual investment in your partner. While it is true that there are investments in work relationships, they pale in comparison to the investments two lovers put towards one another. They are simply just different.

At a basic level, to improve your relationship, you need to build two skills: 1) listening and 2) direct communication. You might be thinking to yourself: "I do these two things very well so I can skip over this part."

WAIT!!

I don't think you do. If you did, you would not be in the situation you are in in your relationship now.

Listening

Empathy goes a long way. The reality is that your partner IS justified in their feelings. Their feelings are their own. Even if you don't understand why they feel that way or you think they are overreacting or they misunderstand a situation, it is the way they feel and their feelings are valid. Effective listeners make great partners, no matter what type of relationship it is. Actively learning to understand where your mate is coming from will not only make you a good *friend*, but it will make you a good *mate*. Listening wholly to your partner is extremely important.

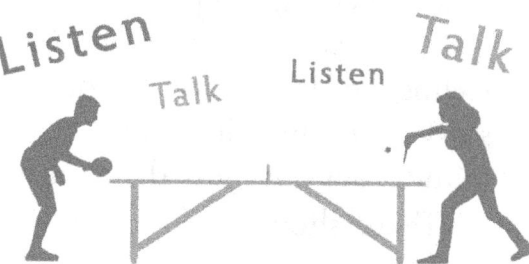

Now, on a slightly more complicated level, to fully understand effective communication, you have to understand that you and your partner try very hard to read each other. Sometimes you are right, but most of the time you are wrong. This is because, oftentimes, we *project* our own feelings onto our "read" of our partner. This is generally called "mindreading" in the therapy field and it needs to stop. To communicate effectively, you must understanding that everything you do sends some type of message to your partner (your body language, tonality, the words you choose, etc.). Think of effective communication as a Ping-Pong game. You are both sending and receiving the Ping-Pong ball. Furthermore, as you should both be listening (ping) and talking (pong), but only when it is your time to talk.

Let's start off with an exercise in basic active listening. Active listening often helps people understand where their partner is coming from.

 Exercise: *"Active Listening"*

Active Listening Exercise

I want you and your partner to tell a brief story about a time something happened to (you) them. Let your partner go first. Let them tell you a story in which they include feeling words and descriptions while they are telling their story. Keep in mind this is a brief story, not under one minute, but not more than five minutes.

There should be only one *speaker* (storyteller) at a

time. The other, the *listener*, remains quiet throughout the story-telling and just listens. When the speaker is done, the listener repeats the story back to them (in their own words), reiterating what they heard. The 1st speaker then tells the listener if he or she is correct. If the listener has actually heard what the speaker said or meant by what they said. Then switch roles.

This exercise is usually a good gauge of whether or not you are a good listener. What I see a lot of is people a) trying to solve their partner's issues while the partner is telling their story, and b) actively responding throughout their partner's story instead of just listening. It is important to note that if you are doing one of these two things you ARE NOT fully listening to your partner or to what is being said. Remember the goal here is to fully listen to your partner with ALL of you. When they are done telling their story your job is not to resolve their issues but rather support and acknowledge their feelings.

2) Direct Communication

I notice couples "dancing around" (as I call it) when they talk to one another. Many get in a very bad habit of not being clear with their wants and needs. Most often we expect our partner to "just know" what we are talking about even though we are not communicating it effectively. After all, WE know what we are talking about, so shouldn't they? Not really.

As a result, when our partner does not understand us, it often becomes the source of frustration and of subsequent conflict. But do not despair, better communication techniques can be learned by both of you. Effective communication includes stating what you want clearly and getting to the point.

If you find that you don't understand what your partner is saying, ask them to give you more information. And/or if your partner is not understanding you, try taking a deep breath and explain your message in a different way. Try not to be harsh or blaming; rather, you need to simply state what you want. Keep in mind that your partner has a right to not want what you want. And you have a right not to want what your partner wants all of the time too. This is where another important skill comes into the picture.

Negotiation

The goal of negotiation is to know your position, learn your partner's position, and come to a mutually acceptable compromise that satisfies both of you. I want to keep this manual simple so I am not going to go too much into the details and many techniques and nuances of negotiation, but I will in a later manual that focuses directly on conflict resolution.

3) Intimacy

Let me ask you (as I ask my clients) a very important question:

What is Intimacy?

I often get a multitude of responses, which is to be expected, so don't worry about your answer; just think about what your definition of intimacy is. It is clear to me how intimacy is acted out within the relationship. As I stated above, I see a distinct difference between males and females and the way they interact within relationships. When it comes to intimacy males often view intimacy as *sexual* and females often view intimacy as *emotional*. The truth is that intimacy can and be *both*. The goal is learning to understand that the meaning of intimacy is different for each person. With that being said, here is your next exercise.

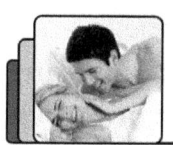

Exercise: *"Intimacy"*

Defining Intimacy Exercise

This is a thirty-minute exercise that will be worth your time. Spend fifteen minutes (individually) discussing what intimacy means to each person. I am instructing you to go "deep" in this exercise. I want you and your partner to know *everything* about what your individual concepts of intimacy are—so much so that when you are finished you will be able to identify what color it is, what it smells like, what it looks like, how you experience it, how you would like to experience it, and so forth.

The goal here is to start consciously considering where you are individually with this concept. It is also about learning how your partner views Intimacy. Ultimately, we want to merge the two ideas so that both of you can experience a new level of intimacy and in turn get your needs met. If you are having a difficult time identifying what intimacy is, ask yourself the following questions:

Based on the working definition of intimacy—"a sharing of thoughts and feelings"—what is/are the barriers to you sharing your thoughts and feelings with your partner?

Are the barriers based on fear? Anger? Trust? Is it that you never learned what intimacy is because you never witnessed or experienced it (your parents/caregivers relationships)? Or is there something else?

Is this your first intimate conversation with your partner? With anyone? If so, relax. Remember, this is a strength-building exercise...it will strengthen your relationship with your partner and that is the goal. Using tact, tell your partner what is going on in your mind when it comes to your thoughts and feelings about intimacy.

The idea of sexual intimacy is a prelude to the next section of this manual on better sex. Sexual intimacy is an integral part of a relationship and it needs to be explored and maintained—especially given some of the differences in the way males and females view the basic concept of intimacy (males connecting "sex" and females connecting "emotional support"). This is a sore subject for couples.

I use a common saying in my practice:

"If a couple is having sex regularly (at least once a week) it's about 10 to 15 percent of their relationship, but if a couple is not having sex, it's a problem that becomes 100 percent of their relationship."

Six Basic Human Needs Principle

I like to work under the following premise: *if you can start meeting each other's' needs, your relationship can flourish.* I often work within the realm of the Six Basic Human Needs Principle (adopted from Anthony Robbins). Keep in mind your opinion of Anthony Robbins is irrelevant. The

concept is of importance. The Six Basic Human Needs are:
1) *Certainty* (comfort and stability: safety)
2) *Variety* (spontaneity)
3) *Significance* (the need to feel important)
4) *Connection/Love* (the need similarity)
5) *Growth* (the need to continually strive for something so stagnation doesn't set in)
6) *Contribution* (the need to make a difference in other's lives)

The idea here is to be able to identify your needs under the above subscriptions You can then start to identify how to get those needs met. With that being stated, the best relationships are able to meet those six basic human needs for each other while understanding that needs will not be met a 100% of the time—there is a healthy balance. But before your partner can meet those needs, you have to identify them within yourself.

 Exercise: *"The Needs List"*

The Needs List Exercise

It is time to identify the 10 needs in a relationship. This concept is different from the Six Basic Human Needs, and knowing these needs will provide a stable foundation upon which you and your partner can rebuild from. The 10 needs will allow you to start looking inward and identifying those things that you need, in general.

Here we go: Each partner should do this individually,

and not necessarily while sitting in the company of the other:

Write down the ten things you feel you need in a relationship to be happy.

Do not focus on your relationship specifically, but rather in general. Do this exercise for your own awareness. Make sure not to focus on your happiness *in relation to* what you think will make your partner happy (as I often see clients do). This is specifically designed to identify what *your* needs are.

After your list is made spend a day thinking about the items on your list in case you want to add or change something. The next day I want you to spend time talking about your needs with your partner, and what each means to you. I also want you to listen to your partner when they talk about the needs on their list.

Now choose at least one of the ten needs on your list and at least one need on your partner's list and each of you try to meet the other's need every day for a week. I want you both to rotate meeting each need on the list throughout the next ten weeks. After 10 weeks have passed, discuss some of the challenges, as well as the positive feelings, you both felt while working on meeting each other's needs. Remember, satisfying relationships are not "me, me, me" oriented. Making an effort to meet your partner's needs is a crucial part of any relationship.

Better Sex

Let's face it: many couples want to have better sex. Better sex begins with good communication skills and a solid understanding of what intimacy is for you and your partner. So now that you have a solid idea of what intimacy means to you and your partner, better sex is right around the corner. Better sex is being present in the moment and enjoying the pleasures of your body as well as pleasing your partner's body. It is often this "being present" that couples have the most difficulty with.

As a culture, we have managed to become amateur porn stars. Faking orgasms and pretending to be more vocal and out of control (as they do in the movies. Women are more prone to this type of façade because they are taught that is what men want. The reality is that it's not true. I have asked, and been told, by countless men what the best sex is for them. Their consistent response is when their partner desires them, when their partner looks like they enjoy sex, and when their partner has a positive look on their face while having sex. I have never heard "when my partner yells and screams and convulses during sex." As a matter of fact, most men view this behavior as mechanical and not as pleasurable.

I teach couples how to remain "present" during a sexual experience. I start them out with the following exercise:

 Exercise: *"Remaining Present"*

Remaining Present Exercise

Whether a couple is having sex or not, this exercise works wonders. I instruct the couple to spend some nonsexual time with one another to reduce anxiety, learn about one another's "hidden zones" (areas of the body that feel good although they are not regularly addressed during sexual intercourse), and remain present. In this sense remaining present means that you are fully aware of all of your senses and actively open to your partner's senses.

I want you to spend two hours a week for two weeks in this exercise. Each partner gets a total of 1 hour a week.

- » Find an area of the home that is comfortable for both of you (both physically and emotionally).
- » Clothes come off (if one or both of you have some body image issues then keep that area covered, but eventually that area needs to become uncovered and the issues need to be confronted.

Massage each other's body from head to toe, experimenting with different pressure during the rub down. Take turns at doing this; it is not meant to be a mutual massage at this point. The first week will consist of four 30-minute sessions (two 30-minute sessions for each of you for a total of one hour a piece). Each partner being massaged needs to allow themselves to feel all of the feelings and sensations on their skin. Do not be surprised if this includes emotionally stimulating sensations as well. Use these thirty-minute sessions to figure out what feels good and what feels not so good. Focus should be on the touch only, not on stress happening in life (in general), but the feeling of your partner's hands upon your skin and the sensations felt. In the first week's session each partner is allowed to direct each other, tactfully, with respect to the pressure of the massage they would like. During the second week, each partner is to remain in total silence during their 30-minute receiving session, focusing only on the body sensations their partner is providing for them.

The goal of this exercise is to teach you how to stay present in the moment. Through this exercise, couples' often learn a very important thing: I can enjoy pleasure brought to my body. It is this platform that allows us to stay present during sex. Once the couple has identified what staying present in the moment feels like, you can learn to translate that into your sexual experiences.

Once you learn how to stay present while feeling pleasure, you can move on to additional exploration with oral sex techniques, sexual positions, and learning how to bring spontaneity back into the sexual component of your relationship.

For this manual, I am going to focus on just one of these. The primary reason is this: if you have followed this manual so far, understanding better communication, identifying intimacy, and learning how to stay present—you and your partner have overcome more than 50% of the issues that have plagued your relationship before. Oral sex and sexual positions can get a little technical, because there are a lot of "side bars" that can be attached to those two. One such example is that some women carry a lot of "baggage" when it comes to oral sex. Though physiologically the clitoris is used only for sexual pleasure for the female many females get caught up in societal messages. Those messages have to do with the vagina being a dirty place, a smelly place, and a place of real insecurity for many women. I have heard countless women state that they are uncomfortable with oral sex for those exact reasons. There are ways to get through that, and I discuss those in other publications. Here I want to stay focused bringing the spontaneity back into your relationship.

Bringing a level of spontaneity back into the sexual relationship seems to be most difficult for couples. In a long-term relationship, couples can get restless and bored—that's no secret. Oftentimes, when couples look back to the beginning of their relationship (the honeymoon phase), they do so with longing and excitement. The big question there is: How did you get from point A to point B (where you were then to where you are now). Part of this can be explained by neurochemicals. You see, in the beginning of your relationship, the excitement factor was fueled by novelty. Novelty allows your brain to secrete chemicals such as dopamine, norephinephrine, and serotonin. Neuroscience has investigated these chemicals in depth when it comes to attraction (the beginning stages of love). Later in the relationship vasopressin and oxytocin move in when there is long term bonding and attachment.

Without getting into a long, drawn-out neuroscience lecture, what I want you to know is that brain chemicals can be manipulated. The levels of dopamine, norepinephrine, and serotonin will eventually balance out as vasopressin and oxytocin move in after some time. Often this vasopressin and oxytocin can be experienced as positive because you and your partner are attached but after some time (which varies between couples) it can be viewed as boring. This is when couples can get restless and bored with one another.

Often this restlessness and boredom can be felt by only one partner while the other has in their mind (usually the woman) the idea of "unconditional love." The reality is that we live in a world where unconditional love takes work. If you are the partner who desires unconditional love, I want you to start thinking about unconditional love in a different way.

Most often, I find people's definition sounds something like this:

I thought he/she would love me no matter what.

This is the fairytale that many of us grow up with. Unfortunately, the fairytale falls short. Love takes work. It takes attention and nurturing. The goal is to make the "work" pleasurable. For example, Mark and Susan come to my office in a relationship breakdown—because Mark is restless and unhappy with their sex-life, because Susan decides she doesn't want to have sex often. She states she is happy and content with the way things are. Meanwhile Mark's needs are not being met physically. Mark meets a woman who is available to meet his physical needs. Mark decides to have an affair with the woman (this is an example of poor choices; I am not condoning affairs). Susan feels betrayed and questions: "I thought our marriage was unconditional love."

Unfortunately, this scenario happens every day. This is what I work to prevent in the relationship. Awareness of a new "unconditional love" is imperative. Unconditional love takes work—first you obtain it; then you have to maintain it. Maintenance—specifically the maintenance of your loving relationship—is needed on the part of both partners within a relationship.

Let's get back to restoring spontaneity to your

relationship. Simple—we will manipulate brain chemicals. Because novelty induces neurochemicals to be secreted, we need to work on that. Don't worry; it's simple. Oftentimes couples get into a routine. You are probably reading this saying, "YUP! That's what happened!" Couple's get into a routine for so many different reasons, i.e.—lifestyle, finances, comfort, etc. The goal is to break the routine by doing novel things. Let's get the excitement back into the relationship.

 Exercise: *"Novelty"*

Novelty Exercise

It's time to brainstorm. Think of, and write down, all those things you have ever wanted to do that are possible to do within your means. Each partner needs to make a separate list (with as many items as possible). Then, sit down over a cup of coffee and talk about it. This is the basis for your future.

You both need to realize novelty doesn't cost a lot of money and it can be very simple to do with just a little imagination. Remember, these novel experiences (anything novel) are the building blocks of fond memories as well. The new experiences a couple has will allow them to look back and say,

"Remember that time we…" thus providing you another shared intimate moment in your relationship.

Where do you usually eat dinner? Do you go out to eat or eat separate (because of work schedules or kids), or do you eat at the kitchen table? At this point I want you both to do something different. Try having a candlelit picnic, outside (if it is warm) or inside wherever if it is cold. Each partner needs to make a dish, or purchase one if you absolutely cannot cook—but I encourage you try, get a recipe. Make it a dish you think your partner will enjoy. Have wine if you are allowed to drink alcohol; otherwise, sparkling water or your favorite beverage will work.

NOTE: try not to amp up on sugary drinks because they will make you crash, which may compromise your sexual behavior with one another (in case the two of you choose to be sexual later). In addition, do not overeat as this will also compromise sexual behavior.

Enjoy yourselves, but don't forget to stay away from sensitive subjects. It is important to stay in the moment. Stay positive, you can reflect, but only on positive things. You can also talk about goals and dreams as long as you remain positive and non-obsessive. The goal here is to have a positive new experience. If you have not done this often then use your imagination to influence it. For example, a lingerie and boxer picnic which can lead to a naked picnic.

Often, when couples get into routine behaviors some of the simplest things are forgotten. It is important to get back to the basics. The simplicity of things can help you and your partner connect again, and again.

Here is a list of novel ideas I have seen from some of my clients over the years:

- » Amusement parks (returns you to adolescent fun!)
- » Hiking/camping
- » Plays and musicals

- » Picking up a hobby together
- » Playing a sport together
- » Taking a cooking, dance, Kama Sutra, etc. class together
- » Playing dress-up as foreplay
- » Getting dressed up (black tie style) and going to dinner
- » Phone sex
- » Teasing each other through text messages (sexually)
- » Having sexual intercourse outside or in the car (even if it's parked in the driveway)
- » Volunteer together (giving back)

The list goes on and on.

Before I end, I want to give you another exercise now that you both have learned better communication skills and learned more about intimacy. You can apply both of these skills to your relationship. Your newly gained basic—very basic—knowledge about neuroscience and the chemicals released by the brain (as mentioned briefly above) will help you and your partner bring some connection back into your relationship. By now, after doing the exercises mentioned above, your relationship should be on a good platform. Here is to a continuing closeness and a better relationship.

 Exercise: "Naked Days"

Dr. Deb's Naked Days Exercise

This is simple. It is time to spend a day, or at least a few hours in a day, naked with one another. It's ok if you have children—trust me. Grab a babysitter for the time—once a month at a minimum; once a week at a maximum. This is a time when the two of you need to be alone.

Do what you would normally do—cook dinner, share a glass of wine, watch a movie, etc., but do it *naked*. Every fifteen minutes or so spend a few minutes embracing one another (at least 30-second intervals) and gaze into each other's eyes (at least 15-second intervals). Do this without having sex. This is not meant to be a prelude to sex but rather a relaxing time to be erotic and be close to one another (yes there is a difference between eroticism and sex).

The goal is to be *close*. It is okay to throw in some passionate kissing (10-second kisses to begin with), but kissing is not necessary to experience enjoyable erotic sensations.

Have you noticed in your relationship that after a period of time partners touching each other starts to decline, eye gazing (caressing your partner with your eyes) declines and even the passionate kissing has become pecks on the lips or on the cheeks. This needs to change. And I hope the exercises help you to change your relationship back to the passion-filled experience you both deserve.

After the "Naked Days" exercise you will most likely feel closer as a couple because you both will have received a surge of a chemical called oxytocin. When you embrace someone for at least 30 seconds you begin to feel closer to them from a brain chemistry perspective. This becomes a great platform to have better sex!

These are the keys to building a loving, trusting, and

well-connected relationship. The above are not one-time exercises. You can continually redo these exercises again and again to stay connected to your partner and energize your relationship in a positive way.

2

Are You Lacking Desire? (Female Edition)

One of the most common sexual functioning issues for women is a lack of desire. Over 50% of women report having issues with desire (and mind you those women are only the ones who are reporting it). The actual percentage is estimated much higher than that. Defining desire and actually finding the ways to help women increase their sexual desire is important for women who want to lead a whole life. By no means am I saying that in order to be happy you have to be having sex. Instead, I want you to identify sex (specifically your sexuality) as an important part of who you are as a woman. Sexuality consists of, not only, sexual desire, orientation, and intercourse, but also self-esteem, personal sense of attractiveness, satisfaction with your whole life, values, beliefs, closeness, and physical connection.

I am not a big fan of viewing female and male sexual desire as inherently different. In fact, I believe that they are quite similar. However, it is important to point out perhaps the most important difference between males and females when it comes to sexual desire: In general, males can have sexual desire independent of biological, psychological, and interpersonal/relational issues, whereas females have a more difficult time separating these things. It is interesting that many women (I have heard this countless times at this point in my career) often report a lack of desire; however, once they start engaging in sex play and/or intercourse, they become aroused and lubricate effectively. This raises some big questions about what is happening with women before sexual intercourse takes place.

Case Study: Sandra

Sandra is a 43-year-old woman. She reports having no desire for sex with her partner. However, she does state that if her partner can get her to the point where she decides to have sex, then once she is engaged in sex she reports enjoying the experience. Sandra states she finds it difficult to initiate sex with her partner, yet she does not have a clear idea why. When asked about what is sexually desirable to Sandra, she reports that romance, and soft touching feels really good. She also states she likes to be cared for and likes her partner to take his time with her. Sandra goes on about the importance of feeling valued for who she is as a person, but also goes into enjoying what she considers to be an attractive person.

What became evident with Sandra was that the things that did make her feel desire were no longer present in her relationship. As a matter of fact, she started to feel like an *object*, which turned her off to her partner.

What Is A Desire Issue?

A desire issue is clinically known as Hypoactive Sexual Desire Disorder or HSDD. HSDD is generally characterized by an absence of both sexual fantasies and desire for sexual activity. In order for this to be characterized as a disorder, the lack of desire has to be present for some time and cause marked distress within the female's life and relationship. NOTE: I do not find it helpful or therapeutic to label these types of issues as "dysfunctions," implying that you are dysfunctional. This is a mindset that from a therapeutic perspective I help you to change. I have all my clients change their language as we know how language and self-talk can be very damaging. Their language on issues like this is changed to a sexual function issue so that the brain has a more positive map to follow. Believe me: it becomes very important in the overall treatment of desire issues and other sexuality issues.

The Causes of a Desire Issue

First, it is important to know that from a clinical perspective: "hypoactive sexual desire disorder" can be:

» *Lifelong/Generalized*: The woman has little or no desire for sexual activity (with a partner or with self-stimulation) and never has since the onset of puberty. There are little or no sexual fantasies and, interestingly, a woman can be orgasmic even though she does not have sexual desire.

» *Acquired/Generalized*: The woman previously had

sexual interest but currently does not. There used to be sexual fantasies and perhaps masturbation, but currently she is lacking sexual desire.
- » *Situational/Generalized*: Little or no sexual desire in specific situations. For example, the woman can have sexual desire for another partner while she is alone, but not with her current partner.

There can also be another subtype of a desire issue "due to psychological issues" such as depression.

There is a chicken versus egg "game" here, i.e. figuring out what came first. For example: *Was it marital issues that led to desire issues or desire issues that led to marital issues?*

When there is a psychiatric issue, such as depression or a medical problem (such as a terminal illness) those issues are dealt with first. Note that sexual functioning issues can lead to a loss of desire and vice-versa. It is important to figure out which issue manifested first. The causes of sexual desire issues in females can be very difficult to understand and pinpoint. This is why I do a detailed history in my office. The first exercise is sorting through exactly what is going on with you. Before we go there I want to discuss a little more about the causes.

Since we are human, we have sexuality. There is NO WAY to deny this. While it is true that people's sexuality is unique to them and that sexual desire is higher and lower in different people—the fact still remains that you are a sexual person. It is a good idea to accept this fact before you go any further. I say this because many women I treat often do not believe they are a sexual person. It is imperative that you recognize this. Below I am going to give you an exercise to help you to see this.

It is also important to realize that sexual desire may not stay consistent throughout life, and that is ok. Stress, children, time management issues, and so much more can be at the origin of desire issues. I often see time management issues as a major root of desire disorders in women, so we will look at that in this manual.

Additionally, there are many drugs that can make a woman lose desire, such as many of the antidepressants. Prozac, Zoloft, and Paxil can cause loss of desire in many women and men. Birth control pills, patches, and birth control rings can decrease desire. Remember that your body is unique and these medications can and do act differently in different people's bodies.

Note: Your first, and one of the most important, things I want you to do is go to your gynecologist and ask for a hormone test. Here are the tests I suggest my female clients get first:

- *Free testosterone:* responsible for overall drive (assertiveness)
- *Progesterone:* too much can inhibit sex drive
- *Estrogen:* more responsible for receptive sex drive, vaginal lubrication
- *Thyroid:* low thyroid hormone can inhibit sexual desire - get the following: TSH, free T3, free T4, Reverse T3, TPOab, and Tgab
- *Cortisol:* it's a stress hormone, indicator to see if adrenal glands are working

Case Study: 46-Year-Old Woman

A 46-year-old woman, married for 22 years, described feeling a diminished sexual desire since her hysterectomy, which was five years earlier. She had never experienced sexual difficulties before the hysterectomy. She had a hysterectomy with her ovaries removed because of excessive bleeding due to fibroids. She was on hormone replacement therapy but she was not on testosterone as one of those replacements. There was no problem with her becoming vaginally lubricated but she reported losing gratification in sexual experiences with her husband. She lost the ability to orgasm regularly with him. When she was given testosterone (she chose to do the bio-identical hormones) she found that her desire returned and her regular orgasms were enhanced.

Beginning Treatment Exercises

Because of the nature of desire issues in females, and how they can be very complex, I often start out very basic (which oftentimes helps tremendously) with women. Therapy tends to revolve around the root cause(s), current issues, and resolution that fit the needs of clients.

It is important to note that the main treatment strategies for Desire Issues are directed at removing the barriers or underlying causes so that the woman can start to feel desire again. Often involved in this treatment is helping the woman to learn how to feel sexual desire again or perhaps for the first time.

Before we get started on some basic exercises there is another thing I want you to identify in your life. Very simply: If you are not exercising I want you to start doing some physical activity. Ideally, I want you to exercise vigorously (where you break a sweat) at least three times a week for 45-minute increments. If there is a health concern that prevents you from doing this then do what you can to get the blood flowing (swimming, sitting in place and moving your arms up and down, whatever you can do!). There is plenty of research that states that exercise improves sexual functioning. One primary reason for this is that it gets your blood flowing and ultimately makes you feel better in many ways such as body image and more energy. I also want you to make sure you are eating a balanced diet with lots of water. Yes, EVERYTHING has some connection to a healthier lifestyle!

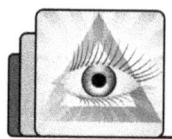 Exercise: *"Self-Awareness"*

As I stated above, I want you to think about the root of your desire issues. Ask yourself these questions and answer them in detail. Note: it is better to write down the answers so you can refer to in the future.

1) Have you ever experienced sexual desire?
2) If you have, when (at what age) did you feel sexual desire?
3) Have you had sexual desire in your current relationship?
4) If the answer is yes, when did you have sexual desire in your current relationship?
5) If you have had sexual desire in your current relationship, when did you notice it start to change

(list the events that you are aware of—i.e. I changed contraception when my partner started yelling at me; when I felt ignored; when I started working more, etc.).

6) When do you currently feel sexual desire (alone, when you are relaxed, etc.)?
7) If you have never felt sexual desire what do you think it feels like?
8) If you have never felt sexual desire, what do you want it to feel like?
9) Do you fantasize?
10) If yes, what is the best sexual fantasy you have ever had?
11) Do you feel tired and overwhelmed?
12) Any history of depression and anxiety? (Note, these issues often need in-office therapy sessions, and that is okay, as it will help you not only with your sexual desire goals, but also in other aspects of your life.)

The answers to these questions are important because they will help you gauge where the issue is stemming from. This is a self-awareness exercise you have to hone in on. It is important to be honest and take some time on this. If your relationship is struggling or if you just can't find the time then your focus is on those areas. After you write down your answers (in detail) look them over and see where the issues are.

 Exercise: *"The Sexual You"*

Accepting you are a sexual person can be difficult. If you are reading this, ask yourself if you truly accept that you are a sexual person. If you say, "Yes I do accept that I am a sexual person," then ask yourself why you will not let yourself experience sexual pleasure.

Sex is not just about intercourse. Sex is about *emotional pleasure*, pleasure of the senses, as well as in most cases relational pleasure. I say in most cases, because there are many people that can have sex outside of a relationship and find great pleasure there as well. Touching, kissing, and other intimate sexual contact can be very pleasing. So take your mind off of sexual intercourse so that the pressure to have sex doesn't create a barrier for you.

Take some time to think about all the ways you are a sexual person. For example, do you like to look nice, do you like to smell nice, do you care about what your body looks like, do you receive pleasure from touch, how do you show yourself love? These questions are just examples that I want you to follow. I want you to list at least ten things that translate into ways you are a sexual person. Then I want you to review them and accept them.

This is a good time for you to open up to your partner. Talking openly about your sexuality (needs, desires, and concerns) can bring you and your partner closer, reduce anxiety, and increase intimacy. Increased intimacy can make both you and your partner enjoy sex more. If your partner is not supportive then there are some relationship issues that need to be worked through in therapy.

In addition to the list above, I also want you to answer the following questions for a bit more of a sensory awareness experience:

1) What emotions do you feel when you are watching a funny movie?
2) What emotions do you feel when you watch a sunset or sunrise?
3) What emotions do you feel when you step on a piece of glass or other sharp object?
4) What emotions do you feel when someone you are in love with gives you a hug?
5) What emotions do you feel when you think of a romantic kiss?
6) What emotions do you feel when you think of a romantic touch (think about different parts of your body: which areas feel the best when touched).

Remember: thoughts trigger emotions and emotions trigger thoughts. Be aware of your thoughts and how they trigger your emotions and vice versa. They can have a role in causing your desire issue.

Getting at the root cause of your desire issues can be a bit daunting because you really do have to identify every area of your life. This is good on multiple levels and for basic self-awareness, since every healthy person needs to understand and enjoy their sexuality. Once you have the answers to some of the above questions you will understand the areas that need to be worked on (i.e., time management, stress, intimacy, better sex skills for both you and your partner, learning how to connect with yourself, etc.)

 Exercise: *"Obstacles to Intimacy"*

The following exercise is one I have all my female clients do when there is a desire issue; sometimes with their partner (if their partner is supportive), but most often alone. I want them to examine their obstacles to intimacy. After completing the two exercises above, this shouldn't be too difficult for you. By now you should have a good handle on the root cause(s), there should be more of an acceptance of you as a sexual person and on a side note, you should have been able to connect with different emotions by answering the sensory awareness questions listed above.

Now I want you to answer the following questions (please do so on a piece of paper so you can come back to this and reflect).

1) When did you initially notice that your sexual desire had changed?
2) Was there something in your life that could be considered a life-changing event at the time you noticed a change in your desire? For example, a death in the family, a realization of some sort, job change, something significant that your partner did that made you feel betrayed, etc.?
3) Think about what your partner is doing that is turning you off. Whether it be: a lack of communication, not the best sex skills, not enough romance and connection, no support, no acknowledgment, he (or she) is overly critical, too passive, too possessive, abusive, habits that turn you off, etc. (you get the

idea). Make a list of these things, think about them for a day or so and sooner than later you will have to discuss the issues with your partner. This is where things can get a bit difficult. Many women have a fear of opening up to their partner. Everything that has been discussed above needs to be discussed with your partner. Support from your partner is very important for a couple of reasons: 1) it allows you to feel safe to explore this aspect of your life and 2) a supportive partner can help you move to the next level by understanding how you feel. In addition, if your partner feels responsible, a discussion can help them understand what you feel.

The goal here is not to *blame* your partner, but rather to identify things that are turning your sex centers off in your brain. I consider open communications about these issues as growth between a couple. No one is perfect and we can all revamp some of the things we are doing. For example, if your partner smokes cigarettes right before trying to engage in sexual activity with you and the smell is revolting to you, this is a habit that can be changed without too much ego bruising. Honest communication is important.

There are a lot of things to uncover within you when you deal with desire issues. Many of these things are mentioned above. However, some of the things that are not mentioned are things like trauma, values, religious upbringing, messages about sex, etc. Ask yourself about these subjects. For example, have you had sexual trauma in your life? What were/are your values around sex? What did your religious upbringing tell you about sex? and What were the messages about sex you received growing up? These are all questions you need answers to so you can address and improve your sexual desire issues.

When we start to uncover your feelings about sexuality, we can move into the touching exercises. I usually put my clients on 6 to 8-week programs of sensate focus depending on the couple. Sensate focus exercises are meant to reduce anxiety and build connection while first building a non-erotic connection. I will end this section here because you have a lot of work to do with the above exercises. Once you finish them you can move on to the next section. Take some time and really do the exercises. Keep in mind that as a female it is important for you to have an emotional connection with your partner. This is the building block for the return of desire. Good luck and keep trying. Increasing your desire is a positive move for you as a whole human being.

3

Are You Lacking Desire? (Male Edition)

The lack of desire has long been discussed in women's sexual health circles, but it is only recently that the lack of desire has been considered with regard to men. It is well understood in the field of sexuality research that desire issues (I do not like the term "disorders") in men are grossly underreported. It is often stated that men suffer from desire issues just as much as females do, if not more. Often male desire issues are treated as erectile "dysfunction" (E.D.), which is erroneous. The prevalence of misdiagnosed E.D. makes sense due to the gender role specifics that men grow up with. For example, men grow up with messages of: "Do not express your feelings," "Be strong," and "Be the 'hunter'" when it comes to sex. This idea essentially removes the humanness from men's sexual identity. There couldn't be a bigger set of myths: that men are always ready for sex and that all of their motivation lies with sexual contact as the end result.

The interesting thing is that desire issues in males will oftentimes cause erectile "dysfunction," therefore a male is often left believing he has a problem with erectile functionality. Many therapists and most medical doctors are not properly educated in this area, so when a male searches for help oftentimes he finds a script for Viagra, Levitra, or Cialis to "cure" his condition. HSDD (Hypoactive Sexual Desire Disorder) is one of the most difficult sexual issues to define and treat because of its complexity. Sexual function issues are mainly treated with a linear model of sexual response. Master's and Johnson's Sexual Response Cycle Model is the primary tool used (still some forty years after its appearance in the mainstream). The major issue with this model is that sexual desire is considered.

Hypoactive Sexual Desire Disorder

Clinically, the lack of desire in both men and women is called Hypoactive Sexual Desire Disorder (HSDD). I simply call this a desire "issue" (rather than a "disorder") to take the pressure and "label" off of my clients. This is so they do not end up feeling inadequate, because this is not about being inadequate. According to the Diagnostic and Statistical Manual of Mental Disorders (American Psychiatric Association, 2000, 2012), the working definition of HSDD is: a persistent or recurrent absence or deficit of sexual fantasies and desire for sexual activity.

The underlying issues responsible for a lack of desire in a male partner can be hormones and psychological problems with partners (it is difficult for men to admit they have resentment or unresolved issues with their partners), major depression, medicines such as some Parkinson's Disease treatments, aging, medical issues (coronary disease, renal disease, decreased sensation in the penis, etc.)

Before I start sounding too clinical, I want to focus on more of a down-to-earth approach and easy-to-understand ideas about working through these issues. Yes, I said, "working through these issues." In therapy we look at all of these issues and start to narrow down the causal factor(s). This is something you can do at home as well. It is time to be aware of the medical and psychological issues you are dealing with. Are you depressed? Do you have a history of depression? Do you have health issues? If so, what are they?

One of the first things I have my male clients do is make an appointment with their urologist to get their testosterone and prolactin levels tested. Testosterone is responsible for sex drive and too much prolactin inhibits sexual desire. We need to know this before we go any further in therapy so that you will understand what direction to take the treatment. So call a urologist. If you have one already, great; if not, there are many to choose from. You can even ask your family doctor to recommend one. Make an appointment and discuss the subject of low desire. They should automatically write you a script for a blood test. If by some chance they do not, request one to get your testosterone and prolactin levels measured.

If testosterone and prolactin levels come back normal and there are no health issues (including medications that you may be on with the side effect of lowering desire like anti-depressants, painkillers, etc.) then it is time to look at psychological/relationship causes. But if the tests indicate low levels of testosterone then before we start considering other issues I want you on some type of replacement for your hormones that your urologist will administer (a prescription).

Again, many things go into the onset of desire issues in men. A thorough evaluation of sexual beliefs, values, religious background, trauma, anxiety, negative thinking, depression, obsessive thinking, social phobias, and panic disorders needs to be performed. In addition, relationship conflict—sometimes related to your thoughts about women in general, as well as your relationship with your mother—can have an effect on your sexual desire.

After you have a clean bill of health and everything physiologically is "normal," begin the following three exercises. But, before that, there is a level of acceptance you need to reach. Note that roughly one in five men have such low desire that they would rather be doing almost anything than have sex. Just because you are a male DOES NOT mean that you are hard-wired for sex—that is a MYTH! It's ok that you are in this situation (that you have a desire issue)—it is human…you are human. The great thing is that you are doing something about it now.

As always, make sure you are exercising at least three days a week for about 45 minutes and make sure you are getting proper nutrition. In addition, make sure you are taking a supplement with at least 11 mg's of zinc in it a day. Zinc does not work in isolation so you need it in a multi-vitamin or even better, getting your vitamins from your food. Zinc fosters testosterone so it helps build sex drive.

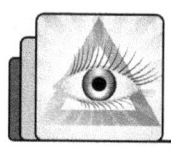 Exercise: *"Self-Awareness"*

Self-awareness is the key to success in so many different areas of your life. Grab a pen/pencil and a pad of paper; then list all those things that cause you stress (as we know stress is one of the biggest desire-killers). This can be anything from work stress, relationship stress, to caring for elderly parents, etc. After you write down the stressors I want you to write down all the ways these things stress you out—and be specific!

For example:

Work: I am stressed out at work because my boss constantly comes down on me and I feel like I can't do anything right. In addition, I work 10-hour days and never get a chance to see my family. That basically makes my wife angry so we fight about time, money, and everything else... (I want as much detail as you possible. There is no limit to how much you write).

 Exercise: *"Connecting with Your Partner"*

Having a supportive partner is a very important component of the treatment process (especially if the relationship has issues such with communication, intimacy, etc.). Ideally, this is the time for you to have a conversation with your partner about how you feel. "How you feel," remember, is not what you think, it is how you really feel. Note that I often have to teach men how to talk with emotion because oftentimes they talk logically rather than in terms of emotions. If this is you then you need to really think about what you feel before you have this important conversation. For example, do you feel disconnected from your partner? Do you feel embarrassed or neglected or abandoned? Why?

Your partner needs to understand where you are with respect to low desire. If you feel like you are not being heard then you need to state that without blaming your partner and that is important here—without blaming your partner. Instead of saying: "You never listen to me," try saying something like: "I do not feel heard in our relationship." If you use blaming words, your partner will instantly go on the defensive and you will not resolve any issues you may have.

Because relationship issues are often at the root of low sexual desire, these conversations need to happen often to aid in increasing your desire. You and your partner may need to redefine what intimacy means to each of you, learn how to communicate better without blame, shame or anger, and learn how to grow together.

There is another exercise I want you to do. Define Intimacy. Both of you sit facing one another, looking at each other, and spend ten minutes talking about what intimacy means to each of you. You can either think about this first or do it "off the cuff," whatever you are comfortable with. This is where we start to identify what each of you needs to feel connected to the other. You may realize that to this point you never gave the concept of intimacy a thought and that you may not know truly what it means for you.

Intimacy is a necessity in a healthy relationship and it is something that is built and can be rebuilt. It is worth the introspection required from both of you.

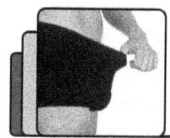

Exercise: "Masturbation Training"

Many men have lost the desire to masturbate. If you have, I want you to slowly start this back up. Think about what you find erotic whether it be thoughts or sensations. If you need a visual this is where a pornographic movie can come in handy (if you are not compulsive with it, porn can be a great tool to get you motivated).

I instruct my male clients to get a pattern of masturbation going at least a couple times a week just to see if you have any desire or motivation for sex. This can often act as the push you need to desire sex again. Keep in mind that if you use porn, it is not based in reality so DO NOT try to reincarnate what you see on the screen. Try not to compare the sex in the porn to the sex you may have had or could have. The sex in porn is not sex in reality. There is a huge level of fantasy in porn movies, which is how they make so much money.

Remember this is for you to get a sense of your sexual desire. If you are partnered and your partner has an issue with you masturbating, this is where another conversation needs to take place. You and your partner are individuals with your own particular needs and ways of learning. This is why a supportive partner is imperative so you can feel ok about your journey in getting your sexual desire back.

4

Erectile "Dys"function Quick Tips

Before we get started, I want to explain why I label this issue Erectile "Dys" function with the quotations around the "dys." I use the quotes because I do not like the word dysfunction. It seems to denote that you are a dysfunctional person. Unfortunately the well-known term for difficulty or inability to obtain or maintain an erection is referred to as this. I would like for you to think of what you are dealing with as simply an erection issue rather than putting yourself into a category of "dys"-functional. Believe me this has a purpose. That purpose is allowing yourself to view what you are dealing with in a more positive light—a more "normal light".

Most men, if not all men, will have some issues(s), at some point in their life, with their penis. Understand this, because once you do you will have overcome a large part of the battle! The reason being is that men, in general, are often preoccupied with this area of their bodies. You are no different. I can guarantee you put a lot of emphasis on your penis, i.e. the size, ejaculation, sexual prowess, and length of time before you ejaculate. The reality of this thinking is that it doesn't allow you to be human. As a human you are not perfect and like many other things on and in the body there are a multitude of things that can affect the function of them. Let's start there—noting that from this point on I will be referring to erectile "dys"function as the erectile function issue.

What is an Erectile Function Issue?

Now that we agree that an erectile function issue and "dys-function" is an issue of difficulty or inability to obtain and/or maintain an erection that is suitable for penetration of the vagina, anus, and/or mouth, we can move forward. Keep in mind that if you experience difficulty occasionally with obtaining or maintaining an erection there may not be any real concern-or alarm as most men, if not all men, will periodically, at points in their lives experience this. Understand this and again you will have overcome an obstacle in your own thinking.

Before we go into the causes and then some of the exercises I use to treat these issues, I want to make something very clear. During the first session with a male dealing with this issue I ask him if he has seen a urologist. If he has, I want to know if anything was abnormal during the visit. If he has not seen a Urologist I send him to one of the urologists I work closely with. Urologists are all over the world so it will be simple for you to look one up in your area. I instruct my clients to let the urologist know they are having erection difficulties so the urologist can do an exam. I also want to see my client's testosterone levels, blood sugar levels, and cholesterol levels since low testosterone, heart disease, and diabetes can cause erectile function issues. Please get these tests. If you do not know what to ask for—ask for a complete blood count including a testosterone level.

I know talking to someone can be awkward, but it is paramount in treating this issue. Keep this in mind: you are not the first one who has had this issue and you are, by far, NOT the last one to deal with it. I tell my male clients: I have heard just about everything, so relax and just tell it like it is. This often reduces some of the anxiety. Remember that your urologist deals with these kinds of issues all day. On that note, your urologist may offer you a script for one of the commonly prescribed drugs for erectile issues such as Viagra, Levitra or Cialis. It's okay; take the script or the samples. I sometimes want men to use these drugs to regain confidence while going through the treatment process. I will explain that a little later.

What Causes Erectile Function Issues?

The causes for erectile function issues can be multimodal. There can be physical causes, psychological causes, and even a combination of the two. The physical causes are generally diabetes, neurological diseases, vascular disease, kidney disease, prostate cancer, some of the surgeries performed for prostate and bladder cancer, smoking, high alcohol usage and drug use, injury, prescription drugs, hormonal imbalances (thyroid, prolactin, testosterone), venous leak, obesity, high blood pressure, Parkinson's, MS,

Peyronie's disease, prostate enlargement, and even blood flow restriction (avid cyclists frequently experience issues due to the bicycle seats restricting blood flow).

Instead of going through these one by one—when you make your trip to the urologist all of these will/should be considered by the doctor. The urologist will ask questions about your health and you need to be honest. Honesty will yield the best end results.

The general psychological causes of erectile function issues are mental health issues such as anxiety and depression, stress, relationship problems, fatigue, guilt, and shame. All of these can have a direct result on the ability to obtain and maintain an erection. Since you are not in my office for therapy, you have to look at these yourself. Ask yourself if you are overly stressed, not happy in your relationship, etc. If you find an area that stands out, to you that will be the area to work on either in therapy or with my manuals.

Additionally, as you age, it may take more stimulation to obtain and maintain erections. Some of this is normal. However, sometimes it can be a direct result of underlying health problems or medications you may be taking as you age. The reality is that if you need a medication to survive, you have to continue on that medication and find ways to still bring sexual pleasure into your life. I help men do this all the time. As a matter of fact, some of the exercises in this particular manual will help with that as well.

Though sex is not and should not be considered the primary glue that holds your relationship together, having erectile function issues can lead to complications. Those complications are generally low self-esteem, relationship problems, stress, anxiety, an overall unsatisfactory sex life, as well as difficulty getting your partner pregnant if you are in a heterosexual relationship and pregnancy is one of your goals. These complications can and oftentimes do feed off one another. For example, not being able to get your partner pregnant can lead to relationship problems, which can lead to stress and anxiety, which can effect one's self-esteem.

Lifestyle

First and foremost we need to take a look at lifestyle—exercise, diet, and stress management. Here is what I want you to do: start exercising a minimum of three days a week for at least 30 to 45 minutes. If you are in good health I want you to exercise vigorously. If you are not in good health, take it easy and build your body's strength back up gradually. I would like you to break a sweat if possible and everyone does so with a different amount of exertion.

Next, I want you to ease up on the processed and grease-filled foods. This means ease up on the pasta, breads, fast food, high fat foods, deep fried foods, and refined sugars (pastries, deserts, ice cream, etc.). I want you to add more protein and more fresh vegetables into your diet. I also want you to start drinking more water. Let's go with the staple recommendation of eight glasses a day. Ease up on alcohol intake as well if you consume alcohol. You should be drinking no more than a couple drinks a week if you want this to work best for you. If you smoke, let's have you cut down as much as possible. Ideally, for the best results, you should work toward quitting altogether. Most men start to feel better from this change in their diet within a week.

If you are taking prescription medications, make sure you go over these changes with your urologist. Some of the medications that can cause erectile function issues are: antidepressants (which ironically can also help in low doses to ease up anxiety), antihistamines, blood pressure medications, muscle relaxers, illegal drugs such as cocaine, marijuana, barbiturates, and methadone. By far, these are not the only drugs that affect your erections, but they are a good list to start from.

Now I want you to identify your stress levels and I need you to be honest with yourself. If you are constantly worried about work, relationships, money, etc., you need to find ways to help manage the stress. Believe it or not, exercise and diet will help reduce stress. Other things that help stress are learning how to breathe properly, journaling, taking at least an hour a day for just YOU, learning how to set boundaries, and understanding that you are only one person. Sitting around worrying about getting things done is only making your situation worse. Learn to prioritize, manage time, and delegate some work to someone else. Though I go over this in depth with my male clients in session, you can do all of this at home by looking at your lifestyle.

In addition, if you are not taking a multivitamin start now. Make sure the multi has zinc in it (as mentioned earlier). Most male vitamins have a good amount of zinc but in general you want to have around eleven (11) mg's a day. Zinc facilitates testosterone and low zinc levels impair prostate function.

Now let's get started with some exercises. Note that these exercises are for males who have psychological issues at the core of their erectile function issue. When it comes to some of the physical causes, my treatment focuses mainly on the many different ways to receive sexual pleasure. Accepting that erectile issues are a normal part of life and changing some of your bad habits including the lack of exercise, diet, and other lifestyle patterns, as mentioned above, is half the battle with erectile function issues. Take a deep breath and relax into yourself.

Exercise One

Start with the pelvic floor exercises,. These are called Kegel exercises. If you are unaware of your pelvic floor muscles, the most basic exercise to work on is learning to stop your flow of urine when going to the bathroom. I want you to stop the flow of urine three times during one trip to the bathroom. I often suggest contracting these muscles anywhere from fifty to one hundred times a day. By stopping the flow of urine you should feel your Pubococcygeus muscles contract. Get familiar with these and every time you urinate stop the flow. You will eventually learn how to contract them without urinating but rather anywhere you are. Another way to do this is by retracting your penis and lifting your scrotum with your pelvic floor muscles. I want these muscles very strong in you because they are the muscles that are around the base of your penis. And they help with maintaining erections.

Exercise Two

If you are partnered, I want you to talk with your partner about how you feel about what is happening. Many times letting go of your feelings can help tremendously by lowering anxiety. Ideally, your partner should be supportive. A supportive partner says a lot about your relationship. The issues *you* are having become an issue *the relationship* is having because simply put: your issue affects the entire relationship. Because of this, your partner can also develop what would be called a secondary sexual function issue (desire issues, arousal issues, etc.). It is VERY important not to blame yourself. These things happen and they are part of a relationship, just like anything else can happen, this is something you both need to deal with. But, then again, that is why you are reading this manual. So let's continue on toward your goal.

Exercise Three

I want you to take a look at your issues with me. Where do you think your erectile issues originate from? This is not a trick question. One thing I encounter a lot is that most men know the origin of their issue, but for whatever reason—fear, anxiety, etc.—they dismiss it rather than confront it. For this treatment to be successful the source needs to be confronted directly. For example, if your partner has rejected your advances in the past or has said something to you that developed a high level of resentment within you—such as "you're not good in bed"—these types of things are often at the source of erectile issues as well as a desire disorder in males.

I need you to be honest with yourself regarding the things bothering you the most. Make a list, and then place the issues in order from the worst issue to the least worst issue so that you can start working on them.

Exercise Four

Answer the following questions: What does the perfect sexual experience look like to you? Imagine: what role do you play? What role does your partner play? Where are you (location) during this sexual experience? What are you saying? What is being said to you? Did you initiate? Did your partner initiate? How do you feel?

This is a guided imagery exercise to help you grow in the direction of getting what you want. Why do I have my male clients do this? Simple: You can tell a lot about what is lacking in your sex life by this simple exercise. This is usually the area I help couples focus on during their sexual experiences together. This exercise allows you to identify some of the areas that need improvement to help you have a satisfying sexual experience (and often your partner as well).

As I stated above, the use of medications like Viagra, Levitra, and Cialis can be used as a backup. Often as a side effect of erectile functioning issues, men lose a sense of self and their sexual self-esteem can drop drastically. Viagra et al can help bring the confidence back. I want to instruct you to use these meds as follows:

If you are nervous about going back in to a sexual experience—the first few times you can use one of these medications if they have worked in the past. For example, if the dose you got from the urologist is 50 mg take one of them the first time you enter back into a sexual situation. The next time cut it in half so you are taking 25 mg. Next, break it into a quarter. The fourth time, use no medication. Be sure to understand that everything else I mentioned above needs to be done before you reach this point. This is ONLY to help you gain a stronger confidence in your sexual performance.

To summarize this discussion: You have a lot of investigative and experiential work to do, but you can do it.

Let's recap:

1) A urologist appointment—to make sure there are no physical health issues and to get your testosterone levels checked
2) A lifestyle change—start exercising, eat better, lay off the smoking, and decrease the alcohol intake; increase zinc, and breathe
3) Do an overall evaluation of your stress levels
4) Do an overall evaluation of your anxiety levels
5) Start your Kegel exercises as described herein
6) Evaluate your relationship
7) Do the Guided Imagery exercise

These exercises are usually enough to do the trick. If you do not get the desired results, chances are you have some deep rooted anxiety issues or relationship issues in which you need to spend some time on. Keep in mind that if you feel you need to do a one on one session, you can schedule with me (in office or via phone) or find a local therapist to deal more with the deeper issues. Good luck and here is to your erectile functions.

5

Getting Control Over Premature Ejaculation

*U*ndoubtedly Premature Ejaculation (PE) is the number one sexual functioning issue that men suffer from. Men of all walks of life can be plagued with this and can suffer great emotional, relational, and mental pain. Historically—and in present day—males wrap a great deal of significance around their penis. This is one of the reasons premature ejaculation and erectile functioning issues are a great source of stress, anxiety, and depression for men. Relax; there is help for these issues. Like any sexual issue, whether it is with a male or a female, work is needed to understand and accept the situation. Figure out the origin, work on obtaining a desired result, and then work on maintaining that result.

Males often suffer in silence longer than they need to because PE, like many other sexual issues males can face, is a source of embarrassment. It is hard for many men to talk about it with anyone, including a specialist. The ironic part is that estimates of one in three men will deal with this issue at some point in their lives. Frankly, I think that males and females deal with sexual issues throughout their lives because a person's sexuality is an integral part of them, but that does not mean these issues are insurmountable.

Before we go any further, I want you to know that I work with this issue very often in my practice. I have seen men who are very embarrassed, very open, and very scared. This is all to be expected. That is why I like to start off normalizing this issue. It is important for you to understand that although it may feel like a big deal to you, in the grand scheme of things, it's really not. Most often, this is a problem that can be fixed. Most men will have some issue with their penis at some point in their lives as the penis is part of their body.

Unfortunately, the penis has somehow become a symbol for masculinity, which on multiple levels tortures men when they have an issue with their penis. Men become so preoccupied with the size, the function, and the look of their penis that when something happens that brings focus to that area, they can start to spiral. Their self-esteem starts to wane and oftentimes so do their relationships. Let's clear up some of that as best we can.

Understand this: You are fine. And without sounding too cliché—you are "normal." As a human male, you will have issues, just as all humans will have issues with other parts of their bodies. Give yourself a break. Drop the embarrassment and shame and let's get you to your desired destination with ejaculation control so you can move forward and enjoy a fulfilling, sex-life.

What Is Premature Ejaculation?

Premature ejaculation is defined, in general, as occurring when a male ejaculates sooner than he or his partner wants him to. Admittedly, this is a loaded definition. Many men wish they could last upwards of 20 minutes after penetration. What is important to note here is the "average" male penetrates for three to five minutes prior to ejaculating. Men can learn to prolong this but it is important to be aware of this average so you don't put undue pressure on yourself. I have had several men come into the office stating that they are suffering from premature ejaculation. My first question to them is always: "What is premature ejaculation?" I ask this specifically because I need to know their understanding of ejaculation control.

Premature ejaculation is less often caused by a physical health problem. Most often it occurs because of anxiety, sensitivity, relationship issues, and feelings of guilt, which I will describe in more detail below.

Over the years I have heard many different things described that I would not consider premature ejaculation; rather, the underlying issue is more often that they have a desire to last longer. I hear things like, "I cum in less than 30 minutes."

This is something I want to clear up with you before we go any further. There is a difference between (1) wanting to learn more control and (2) actually having premature ejaculation. That difference is a marked inability to meet the "average" time before ejaculation.

But consider this: "A problem isn't a problem unless it's a problem."

What this means is that if your partner is happy with the length of time and can perhaps not go any longer, then there may not be a problem at all. In fact, if they go any longer, there may become a problem. There are really no clear, exact time limits here. The diagnosis of premature ejaculation is based on the following: "When [early] ejaculation causes marked distress in your relationship."

The exercises that follow will help you with *both* premature ejaculation and learning control over your ejaculation. These are tried and true in my practice. I use them with my male clients on a daily basis.

What Causes Premature Ejaculation?

Before you get to the exercises, I want you to think about your history with anxiety. Look back on your life and determine, on a scale of 1 to 10, the amount of anxiety you feel you have (if any). If you are unsure, a partner is a good person to ask about this as they can oftentimes see things in us that we cannot see in ourselves. I want you to make a mental note of the first time you felt anxious feelings and think back to exactly how those feelings felt. Do you still feel them? When do you feel them? How often? I need you to really think about whether or not these feelings have prevented you from doing any of the things you ever wanted to do or prevented you from doing things to the best of your ability.

As anxiety is often partially to blame for premature ejaculation, it is imperative to examine anxiety within yourself. You can write it down as a release or you can talk about it with a caring partner. This is one of the first steps in the process of overcoming premature ejaculation. Some of the most common anxieties prompted by the idea of sex include the fear of being judged as inadequate by a partner and/or oneself, which could include negative thoughts about penis size or the inability to control ejaculation as well as "spectatoring."

Definition

"Spectatoring" – focusing on your performance—often from a third party perspective—and loosing site of pleasure.

Anxiety about *intimacy* can also be a concern, albeit sometimes an unconscious worry. Although it is much different than premature ejaculation, I have seen men condition themselves to not ejaculate (delayed ejaculation) due to not wanting to fully commit to their partner, or due to a fear of getting her pregnant. The point is that anxiety can be the root cause of many issues with sex in men. Performance anxiety is connected to this general anxiety concept. Men who are overly concerned about ejaculating too early (as they see it) or not being "good" at sex can internalize sex as a performance. Ironically, because of these anxious feelings, men will ejaculate earlier—reinforcing the anxiety and affecting their experience.

Another VERY important step is to visit a urologist just to make sure (even though it is less common) there are no underlying physical/health issues. For example, injury, hormonal issues, effects from medications, inflammation of the prostate, abnormal levels of brain chemicals called neurotransmitters, or smoking. After all, improving you and your partner's sexual experiences is so important you don't want to overlook something.

Other Causes of Premature Ejaculation

After considering your anxiety levels, I want you to think about some of these other common causes of premature ejaculation. It is most helpful to hone in on the exact cause(s) so we have a solid platform (understanding) to treat the issue. So far, we looked at anxiety and the less common possibilities of one or more physical health issues. But there are other possible causes of premature ejaculation:

1. Patterns Developed with Early Sexual Experiences

It is no secret that young boys find their penises interesting and arousing at the same time. Before puberty hits, young males will bring themselves to an erection and feel the physical pleasure of the sensitivity of their penis. Boys usually do not ejaculate until they have reached puberty because their prostate has not fully developed. With the push of hormones (androgens) the prostate matures and the pubertal male can then ejaculate.

Ejaculating is a newfound sensation of excitement for young males. Yet, males often become concerned about being "caught" experiencing so much pleasure. This is essentially the beginning of conditioning yourself to climax too quickly. There are several things that go into this caution, such as the messages our families give us about sexuality, religion, and other factors that may include shame and embarrassment. The end result is that sometimes males end up conditioning or training themselves to ejaculate quickly so no one "catches them" bringing pleasure to themselves. When they enter into their first sexual relationship, this pattern often follows them. If a young man feels a sense of disappointment from their partner, often their sense of self can feel damaged. This again can travel with him into his adult years.

2. Guilt, Shame, and Depression

Guilt is one of the most unpleasant emotions we, as humans, have to experience. Guilt, shame, and premature ejaculation are tied together in an interesting way. Guilt and shame often stem from childhood experiences, which may be considered negative, embarrassing, and traumatizing. This often begins when we are scolded for sexual curiosity or caught masturbating as a child and confronted by a caregiver in a negative way. In addition, guilt and shame can come from societal standards that specify the "appropriate" age to have sex. Undoubtedly, there is no set age for sex to begin. Yet if a man has reached his mid-twenties (or older) and has not had sex, there can be a tremendous amount of guilt and shame stemming from the resulting anxiety to have sex.

Definition

"**Hypoactive**" — abnormally inactive. Contrast this to 'hyperactive,' which means: abnormally active.

3. Depression

When we experience depression, many things can happen. Sexual issues often go hand-in-hand with depression—issues such as erectile dysfunction, *hypoactive* sexual desire, *hyperactive* sexual desire, and yes, even premature ejaculation. When a male is depressed—suppose his sexual desire is intact but he has lost the common interest in most other life tasks—often he will have ejaculation control issues. To compound this, premature ejaculation will often lead to erectile dysfunction (see chapter 4); conversely, erectile dysfunction can often turn into premature ejaculation. As confusing as that sounds it is true that there is often a negative feedback loop with these two bodily reactions. Just like anxiety can lead to depression and depression can lead to anxiety so are premature ejaculation and erectile dysfunction interrelated.

4. Hypersensitivity

Some men are born with hypersensitivity while other men teach themselves to be overly sensitive through early masturbation. Learning how to control the hypersensitivity through the exercises below will help with this. You can also use condoms to help decrease sensitivity. Furthermore, it is important to experiment with sexual positions with a partner to find those positions that do not have as much friction on your penis; this will help delay ejaculation. In actuality, oftentimes switching positions can help prolong ejaculation because it essentially refocuses thinking.

5. Relationship Problems

Note that with males who ejaculate prematurely, I often see a lack of education around a multitude of issues in their relationships. For example, male and female sexual response, anxiety about sexually transmitted infections, anxiety about poor sexual performance, and a marked difficulty in identifying their own sexual self. In addition, there are interpersonal relationship issues with the partner. I often see men whose partners are non-supportive, ridiculing, uninterested in sexual pleasure themselves, and who threaten to leave the relationship because of the premature ejaculation issue. All of these behaviors are not only anxiety and fear producing but they are also dehumanizing. It is unlikely that your premature ejaculation issue will improve until your partner identifies their own issues and deals with them either in individual therapy or couples therapy.

Treatment Strategies

Premature ejaculation can be treated in many different ways. Oftentimes a combination of various approaches works best. As I stated above, a trip to the urologist is imperative. Before we start working on treatment strategies, I want you to be sure there are no medical issues at the origin of your premature ejaculation. If that is the case, you need to take care of those issues first and then we can start working on the "leftover" issues.

If there are no medical issues, we can start with the goal of increasing your ejaculation control. For example, if you are currently ejaculating after about 20 seconds and you tell me you want to last one hour—your goals may be set too high. That doesn't mean you will not get there, but let's start off a bit more conservative and get you to three minutes, then five minutes, then seven minutes, etc. At that point you will have the tools to train yourself to last longer.

After we look at your anxiety levels as stated above, I want to know what your lifestyle is like. How much do you exercise? How much alcohol do you drink? What is your diet like? What are your stress levels? Ideally, I want you exercising, at least three times a week for 30 to 45 minutes (making sure to break a sweat). Exercise helps you in many ways; not only with premature ejaculation issues but also with those other sexual issues discussed earlier in this book. Diet is also beneficial; I want you eating a balanced diet with high protein so you have energy. Lower your alcohol intake to no more than three drinks a week. I want your stress (work, life, etc.) managed. Managing stress is often the difficult part, and a topic on which we spend a lot of time in therapy. Since you may not be present in the office with me, I want you to take a good look at your life and determine where you can make some changes—positive changes, so you have more time to relax and de-stress. Reduced stress enables more time for sexual pleasure.

For Those in a Relationship

It is very important to take a look at your relationship (if partnered). If you are partnered, it is imperative that your partner be part of this process. There is NO DOUBT that when one person in a relationship has a sexual issue, it becomes *the relationship's* issue. I can't stress this enough. Treatment for sexual issues and concerns works the best when 1) the person with the issue is open minded, 2) the person with the issue is motivated for success, and 3) the person with the issue has a supportive partner (when partnered). This support provides a loving, supportive environment in which to work through this issue, and this increases the success rates tremendously.

Exercise: "Deep Breathing"

Learn how to take deep breaths. As simplistic as this sounds most often individuals with anxiety issues forget how to breathe. Inhale through your nose. Hold it in for five seconds, and blow it out through your mouth feeling it in your abdomen as you let your breath out all the way. Repeat this 10 times right now. The goal is for you to learn what it feels like to relax. Breathing allows your brain to receive much needed oxygen, which is important when dealing with anxiety-based issues.

Exercise: "Kegel Exercise"

All of my male clients learn about Kegel exercises. Start them now. The way you learn how to do Kegel exercises is to, while urinating, stop the flow of urine a few times during urination. You will feel your pubococcygeus muscles contract, which are often called your "PC muscles."

The Sexual Response Cycle

In this exercise, I treat PE on the basic model of sexual response. Traditionally, there are four phases of sexual response, which include: Excitement, Plateau, Orgasm, and Resolution (adapted from Masters and Johnson).

Phase 1: Excitement

The general characteristics of the excitement phase, which can last from a few minutes to several hours, include the following:

- » Muscle tension increases
- » Heart rate quickens and breathing accelerates
- » Skin may become flushed (blotches of redness appear on the chest and back) generally called "sex flush"
- » Nipples become erect (for both men and women).
- » Blood flow to the genitals increases, resulting in erection of the man's penis
- » The man's testicles swell, his scrotum tightens, and he begins secreting Cowper's gland secretions or "pre cum"

Phase 2: Plateau

The general characteristics of the plateau phase, which extends to the brink of orgasm, include the following:

- » The changes in your body beginning in Phase 1 are intensified
- » The man's testicles are withdrawn up into the scrotum
- » Breathing, heart rate, and blood pressure continue to increase
- » Muscle spasms may begin in the feet, face, and hands and other parts of the body depending on the person

Getting Control Over Premature Ejaculation

» Muscle tension increases

Phase 3: Orgasm

The orgasm is the climax of the sexual response cycle. It is the shortest of the phases and generally lasts only a few seconds. General characteristics of this phase include the following:

» Involuntary muscle contractions begin
» Blood pressure, heart rate, and breathing are at their highest rates, with a rapid intake of oxygen
» There is a sudden, forceful release of sexual tension
» Rhythmic contractions of the muscles at the base of the penis result in the ejaculation of semen
» "Sex flush" may appear over the entire body

Phase 4: Resolution

During resolution, the body slowly returns to its normal level of functioning. Before a man can become erect again there is a refractory period which can last anywhere from 10 minutes to days, depending on the individual male.

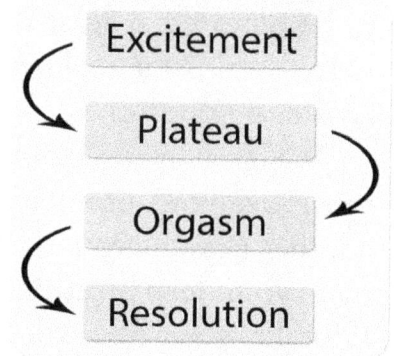

This gives you a brief idea of the sexual response cycle in men. I am treating premature ejaculation on the Plateau phase of this cycle. Once you are sexually excited you enter into the plateau phase, which in men with premature ejaculation issues is very short. Often a man with premature ejaculation issues goes right from excitement into orgasm. Your goal is to extend the plateau phase. You are going to do this through masturbation first.

 **Exercise:** *"PC Muscle Flex"*

I want you to go somewhere where you have some privacy so that you are not anxious about someone walking in on you. This is really important, especially if you have shame or guilt as well as anxiety to work through. I want you to think of a sexual scene that excites you. I want you to bring yourself to a full erection and then stop masturbating. Wait fifteen to twenty seconds and bring yourself to full erection again. While you are waiting your fifteen to twenty seconds I want you to flex your PC muscles that you became familiar with the Kegel exercise. I want you to repeat this three times before you allow yourself to ejaculate. This is to be repeated at least three times a week for a period of four weeks. Your goal here is to become very aware of your "point of no return."

When you are comfortable with this exercise, you can move your partner into the treatment. Since having another person around often builds anxiety you will need to do your deep breathing exercises during this time. Note: If it takes you a little while to control your body that's OK. Do not get discouraged; just continue doing the exercises. Remember: this is a retraining process, and it will be worth your efforts.

Exercise: "PC Muscle Flex Redux"

Repeat everything in exercise two but this time your partner will be manually stimulating you in the same way and for the same duration as mentioned above. This can become a good part of the sexual experience with your partner. Invite them to join you, ask them to help you as they are / will be part of your sexual life.

Exercise: "Sexual Intercourse"

Everything you have learned so far now gets transported into sexual intercourse. However, it is you and your partner's responsibility to find the position(s) where you have most control. Often this is partner on top so when you are getting close to ejaculating you can control your partner's movement by holding the hips of your partner still. However, your partner should be instructed to go slow. You need to be able to say to your partner "slow down" or "stop" if you are getting too excited. After all, this is for the mutual benefit and pleasure of both of you.

This is a very simple series of exercises to begin with. These exercises often help men control premature ejaculation. One thing I always tell my male clients is to think positive. If you have it in your mind you are going to fail, then you will. Consequently, if you have it in your mind that you will succeed and gain control, extend your erection time, and stave off your ejaculation, then you will.

In Chapter 1, *Improving Your Relationship One Step at a Time*, I talk about being present and learning how to accept pleasure. When dealing with premature ejaculation, it is important that you learn how to enjoy the extended feelings of pleasure brought to you by holding off your ejaculation. I often instruct my couples to do sensate focus exercises, which can take upwards of six weeks. However, you can get the gist of sensate focus exercises if you take some time and do the following exercise:

Exercise: *"Sensate Focus"*

For two weeks I would like you and your partner to spend 30 minutes apiece, twice a week for a total of one hour a week for each of you, naked. While you are naked I want you to spend the first thirty minutes massaging your partner while staying away from the genitals, anus, and breasts. This is meant to be a non-erotic exercise. The goal is NOT to have sex and take away pressure for sex. After those thirty minutes, your partner is instructed to do the same for you: massage your body without touching your genitals, anus or breasts. This exercise is to help you understand staying present and learning how to receive pleasure in a non-sexual way. Focus on the sensations on your body only.

The above exercises are a staple of my practice when I deal with premature ejaculation. Of course there are some deeper issues that can be at the core of premature ejaculation, which may need more serious therapy. These can be trauma (all kinds, but usually sexual), values, religious beliefs, anger for females, lack of social skills, and serious relationship issues, to name a few. Try the above exercises first. If you have relationship issues, you may want to pick up my relationship manuals and complete the exercises in those too so you and your partner can start to reconnect.

Good luck and here's to extended sexual pleasures.

6

How to Talk to Your Young Children About Sexuality

It's never too late to talk to your children about sexuality! While it is better to have discussions with them earlier in life than later, the communication and open dialog is paramount to a child's development. Every moment in a child's life can be a "teachable" moment and this is really what I want you to take away from this section.

Children are curious and children are sexual beings with questions that deserve answers. You, as their parent, need to be the one that guides your child through their development, yes even their sexual development. You can rest assured that your child will come into contact with sexual decision making with age. It's up to you to prepare them.

To begin with, I want to clear something up with regard to the definition of sexuality. People often think the definition of sexuality is how or why people have sexual intercourse. Sexuality is more of a human expression and it consists of so many different components. The following is a definition from the World Health Organization:

Sexuality is a central aspect of being human throughout life and encompasses sex, gender identities and roles, sexual orientation, eroticism, pleasure, intimacy and reproduction. Sexuality is experienced and expressed in thoughts, fantasies, desires, beliefs, attitudes, values, behaviors, practices, roles and relationships. While sexuality can include all of these dimensions, not all of them are always experienced or expressed. Sexuality is influenced by the interaction of biological, psychological, social, economic, political, cultural, ethical, legal, historical, religious and spiritual factors.

While it is true that children do not have to know all of this at a young age, one thing that I have seen over and over again is that most parents need a solid definition for themselves of what sexuality means before they can comfortably discuss it with their children. Our education often comes from our own parents and is passed down through the generations. It is important for parents to understand that sexuality is so much more than just the *physical* act of sexual intercourse. Sexuality, in fact, spans across everyone's life. It can be as subtle as body image and self-esteem and as diverse as what healthy relationships look like. That is where we will begin the education in this section.

Sexuality, though we all possess it, is in some sense developmental. What I mean by this is there are appropriate topics to discuss with different ages and stages of our learning process with regard to the education of sexuality. For example, a child of age five does not need to understand the inner workings of oral sex or for that matter intercourse. However, he or she does need to understand that mommies do get pregnant and the baby is held in the uterus (belly). This is generally what is referred to as Developmentally Appropriate.

A top question I hear about sex education in childhood is Why? Why do children need to learn about sex? This underlies a common misunderstanding. Remember your education of your child is not about the *physical* act of sex it is about *sexuality*. Teaching about sexuality can help a child understand him/herself. The education can also help a child cope with peer pressure, understand their bodies, have loving relationships, positive self-esteem, and ways to protect themselves from sexual predators. Education at a young age is often frowned upon. However the research supports that children grow up more aware about who they are as human beings when their education about sexuality begins earlier rather than later. It is clear that sexuality education DOES NOT lead to early sexual experimentation.

Children get sexual messages early on from the media, by what parents say and do, by what their peers or siblings say and do, and even by the words we teach them for their body parts! I find it interesting that the words hoo hoo and pee pee are remotely still acceptable. What do you think children are learning when their parents can't even bring themselves to say the words penis and vagina? We are teaching them embarrassment and shame.

Most parents find talking about sexuality with their

child a dreadful day. While we know one day isn't remotely enough for this lifelong discussion it is still referred to as "that day." If parents can't bring themselves to talk about sexuality look at the message they are sending children. I like to think of life encompassing countless educational moments. With regard to sexuality education, those educational moments can be brought to life watching a television show or even a cartoon. Let's take cartoons for example:

I'll never forget watching Tom and Jerry, as a child of maybe six years old. I loved the simplicity of the colors and the characters. Tom would chase Jerry and always wound up getting hurt in some way. I would watch it for hours! Occasionally, there would be this white female cat that would prance in front of Tom shaking her tail (mind you she was very curvy—huge message in that!). I remember thinking about the concept of boyfriend/girlfriend as well as what's going on?

When I think back on those moments, I realize there was an educational moment there but my parents were unable or unwilling to open the floor up for discussion. In my profession, currently, I often reflect on these moments and similar moments and realize how great it would have been to hear things like:

"Awww look Deb…Tom has a crush on that pretty little cat. Do you know what a crush is?" or at least I could have asked what a "crush" was.

"That's so cute; they might be boyfriend and girlfriend." My parents could have even left it open for me to ask, "What is

a boyfriend..." Or they could have asked: "Do you know what a boyfriend and a girlfriend are?"

These two simple questions could have spawned a conversation about what a healthy relationship looks like as well as diversity in relationships due to the fact that Tom was blue and the female cat was white (depending on the developmental readiness of the child and their age). My parents, like many others, never took these types of opportunities to open the door and build the trust that their kids could ask them about any subject. I don't want you to make the same mistakes my parents did. Learning things on my own was not fun, but more importantly—it was dangerous.

I want you to learn how to make as many moments as possible educational moments so your children can grow up with the knowledge they need to have:

1) Understanding relationships
2) Liking their body
3) Understanding how their body works
4) Being able to talk to their parent(s) openly about anything
5) Feeling comfortable within themselves: ALL aspects of themselves

Key concepts of sexuality education involve teaching:

1) People make choices
2) It's OK to be curious
3) Your body is wonderful
4) Respect—of self and others
5) Families can change

6) Differences are positive

Sexuality, as part of being human, is the mind-set that you will want to adopt to be ultimately effective. Think about it: human beings, just by the mere fact of being human, are sexual creatures. We have natural hormones that do produce sexual feelings, make us feel good and control aspects of our sexuality—like breast feeding, lubrication, erections, and much more. Besides that we are surrounded by messages—many of which are inaccurate—in our environment that you do not have any control over as parents. These things include your children's peers, billboards, magazine covers in the grocery store, and advertisements on TV, radio, and the Internet. While you may think you have control over the television, computer, and the music your child listens to, unless you grow your children in a bubble you will need to remember they do interact with their peers. Point being, they may not be able to listen to a certain type of music in your home but what they listen to with their friends may be quite different. It is your job to help balance this out with education and guidance.

If you find that you can't bring yourself to say words like penis and vagina then you may have your own personal issues to resolve, but I want you to remember this: these are not dirty words; they are, as a matter of fact, clinical, proper words for that which your children and you possess. Reading up on sexuality education related material may help you to break down some of those walls. Keep in mind if you are uncomfortable talking about sexuality with your child then chances are they will become aware of your discomfort. You are sending a clear message with your discomfort. That message is *sexuality is uncomfortable!* And it does not need to be. Before you start the education process with your child I recommend you read a book like *Guide To Getting It On* by Paul Joannides. This book is a fun and easy to read book that is known to capture adult's attention with regard to sexuality. It's one of the "bestselling" books on sexuality!

Tolerance is a big part of how children form their own personal sexual identity. Creating an environment that is tolerant and nurturing of whole-body sexuality is important to the success of a positive sexual identity. This includes many of the things already addressed but also includes values and non-judgment. In general, children can be very hurtful when dealing with peers, so teaching your child about sexuality in a positive non-judgmental way allows them to understand diversity. Whether you like it or not we are a diverse population, and the more you teach your child to single out others the more they will question their own identity and sense of self. For this reason it is important to educate your child with the facts of diversity and teach them that every human on this planet has a place and that we are all part of a larger community.

We know that children have A LOT of questions about A LOT of things. Sex is merely one of those things that they have questions about and are curious about. This is normal and appropriate. It happens to all of us. It happened to you. How you respond to their questions is paramount. Remember, teaching about sexuality in the early years has little to do with the physical act of sexual intercourse. It has more to do with creating a platform of a child's healthy self by helping them develop physically, mentally, and socially in healthy and stable ways. And if you establish an environment in which your children can come to you with any question because you are open to discussing "anything" with them, then you open the communication doors in your relationship with your children. A great building block in life.

Some Guidelines to Follow

Sexuality Education geared to the child's development level

Though children are smart and intuitive they are unsophisticated in their thinking. Most often they think in purely concrete ways. This means they are not concerned with details and for that matter may not even be able to understand details. They are concerned more with *what, where,* and *how.* For example, how does a baby get inside the stomach? Where do babies come from? There is no need to go into detail about sexual intercourse—rather simply answer their questions as honestly and developmentally appropriate as possible. I'll give you some examples in a bit.

Less is Better

Because you are an adult, you may lean toward giving a more complicated answer than is needed. Keep in mind what is stated above. Then start out with a simple answer and only go further if your child continues to ask more questions.

The difference between adult and child sexuality education.

Make sure you distinguish between what you know and what your child should know. A common mistake, for example, is if a parent sees their five- year-old child on top of another child they think the children are trying to have sex. This is the way adults often understand this behavior, yet the five- year-old is most likely mimicking something they either saw you do or something they happened to catch on television and it has not one thing to do with sexual intercourse as children of this age do not understand this concept.

Your goal is to not be too *reactive*. Remember, you are helping your child develop a healthy sense of themselves, not preparing them for a disaster. Be careful not to focus your energy on making sure they don't have sex, get pregnant or contract a sexually transmitted infection. This education will come later, when they are older.

Common questions from five and six-year olds and the best, age-appropriate responses

Where do babies come from?
"Mommy has something called a uterus. It's a warm and cozy place inside my body and it holds the baby."

How does the baby get in mommy's stomach?
"Females are born with little eggs, one of them is called an ovum. That egg needs a little help from daddy. A man has something called sperm. When the sperm meets the ovum, the baby starts to grow."

Why don't I have a penis (pee pee, wee wee, etc.)?
"All girls have a vagina and boys have a penis. Boys and girls have a lot of similar things on and in their bodies but some things are different. Both boys and girls are very

special."

Why do you have hair down there?

"Both males and females get what is called pubic hair when they start to mature. This can begin to happen around age ten. The pubic hair protects the vagina and the penis."

As we move up in age the questions get a little more specific, and that is ok. Around age seven and eight, children are learning more and maturing. They are also seeing more in things within their environments, which is critical.

How does the baby come out of mommy's stomach?

"When the baby is ready, which is usually about nine months after it began growing in there, the baby comes out between mommy's legs. There is an opening between mommy's legs which is called the vagina."

You can also go further at this point and do an educational lesson on the vulva and penis if your child seems interested. Note: It also doesn't hurt to ask if they want to know more. Oftentimes, they will not and that is OK. This means you have to know what they both are and what they are used for.

The Vulva consists of the external genitalia of females. It includes the labia minora (inner lips) the labia majora (the outer lips), the mons (the fatty pad where the pubic hair grows), the clitoris, and the opening of the vagina.

The Penis is a biological feature of the male that is used for urinating and semen flow.

What is sex?

"The term sex is often used interchangeably with sexual intercourse. Sexual intercourse is when a man puts his penis into a woman's vagina. Two adults have sexual intercourse to show love, attempt to get pregnant or to feel good" (notice the key word here is *adults*).

What is sperm?

"A sperm is something males have. They are cells that meet the female's egg and together the sperm and egg create a baby. Sperm is carried in white liquid called semen so the sperm can get out of the man's body."

At ages eight, nine, and ten—oftentimes children's questions become more life-oriented as they start to see their friends having stepparents or see their parents go through divorce. Questions can begin to revolve around marriage and relationships. Questions about relationships may pop up.

What is divorce?

"Divorce happens when two married people choose not to be married any longer. They may still love each other but feel as though they would be happier if they were not married. They still love their children and their children still love them. It's just that sometimes some relationships do not last forever."

But the curiosity about sex continues…

Is it bad if I have sex?

Most children are curious about what sex is. And most children feel good about waiting until they are older to experience sex and all of the emotions that come with it. (Notice that you are staying neutral here).

However, it's never OK for an older child or an adult to touch you in sexual ways. This is *manipulation* of a child by an adult. If you ever hear of something like this happening or if it happens to you be sure to tell me or another adult so we can make sure it stops.

By now children are aware of the words "gay" and unfortunately many of the other negative words that surround orientation.

What is a faggot?

A faggot is a very mean word that some people use to hurt a male who falls in love with another male. But its true definition is a bundle of sticks or a cigarette.

How do two women have sex?

In much the same way that a male and female do; there is touching and kissing and other ways to make each other feel good and show love. Because a female does not have a penis and sperm the sex is a bit different than what we have previously talked about.

How do two men have sex?

In much the same way that a male and female do; there is touching and kissing and other ways to make each other feel good and show love. Because a male does not have a vagina the sex is a bit different than what we have previously talked about. (Very much the same as the discussion as two females).

Though these may seem like hard questions to answer, communication is paramount for children to develop a healthy sense of themselves and their sexuality. Along with communication, you should try to have a relaxed body language and a positive look on your face so your child does not sense any negative feelings within you. This will also help your child learn that they can come to you and openly discuss any subject, large or small.

Another approach to sexuality education with your child is teaming up with another parent and discussing sexuality education. If the two (or more) of you can be on the same page it is possible to do a group educational session. If this is done it is always a good idea to add in a warm-up exercise. A warm-up exercise is a way to break the ice and get everyone lighthearted about an otherwise "heavy" subject. Scavenger hunts are great for this! And you can be as diverse as you want depending on the age of the children.

Diversity Scavenger Hunt

Parent(s): write down a list of things that can be applied to children. Examples are "Find someone who lives with just mom," "Find someone who is an only child," "Find someone who likes to eat ice cream." Make a copy of this list for all the children involved (including yourselves).

Pass out the lists and have children go around and ask the other kids and adults present if they like or have what is on the list. If they do they get to write their name next to it. Be sure to bring colored pencils or crayons!

This is just a guide as you move your way toward getting more comfortable yourself with sexuality and the basics. As children age, you want to be the go-to person for their questions. As children turn into teenagers, you will have to be armed with the knowledge. A book like *Guide To Getting It On* by Paul Joannides, as mentioned above, can be a fun and educational way to educate yourself and your teen!

Summary

Many couples just need a little assistance to overcome incompatibilities, and this assistance often falls into three areas: (1) better communication, (2) increased intimacy, and (3) better sex. Improvements in these areas can positively affect a relationship, and the resulting changes will not take place overnight; rather, they occur when couples take many small steps.

There is a basic difference between "intimacy" and "sexual intimacy." Sexual intimacy involves more than intimacy: In addition to the sharing of thoughts, feelings, goals and hopes, with sexual intimacy, there is a mind, body, and spirit connection. If this connection is not present, sexual intimacy may be lacking.

People enter relationships because they have a basic human need to "connect." There are common signs in a struggling relationship. They include (1) physical and emotional distance, (2) a lack of enjoyment in each other's' company, (3) negative comments made to one another, and (4) an increase of arguments with a lack of resolution. Relationships are generally improved by better communication and increased intimacy. Couples can engage in various exercises—as outlined herein—to help improve an ailing relationship.

For women, a lack of desire is a common issue related to sexual functioning. The clinical name for this is Hypoactive Sexual Desire Disorder (HSDD). This condition can be a lifelong disorder or can occur during an interval in life. In addition to stress and other factors, drugs can be the root cause of HSDD. Prozac can decrease desire, for example. For men, who suffer from a lack of desire just as much as women (if not more), a lack of desire goes largely unreported, which is possibly an artifact of societal expectations. A common myth is that all men are perpetually ready for sex and able to perform on an instant's notice. Testosterone and prolactin levels play an important role in the desire of males: while testosterone increases sex drive, too much prolactin inhibits sexual desire. As with women, desire levels in men can be affected by stress and other factors. Exercise and nutrition are also important to maintaining proper levels of desire.

Erectile function (or "dys-function") relates to the difficulty or inability to obtain and/or maintain an erection suitable for penetration of the vagina, anus, and/or mouth. This disorder can have physical causes, psychological causes, and even a combination of both. Diseases such as cancer, diabetes or neurological disorders can cause erectile dys-function. Other physical factors such as smoking, alcoholism, or hormonal imbalances can be a factor. The problem may also be psychological. Anxiety, depression, fatigue or other psychological states can lead to erectile dys-function.

Notes

Printed in the USA
CPSIA information can be obtained
at www.ICGtesting.com
CBHW072140270924
15059CB00005B/60